CONTENTS

Cover design by S. L Salvador Jr.

Chapter 1

The Fam

Twinnie walks over to the mailbox. She grabs the mail start shuffling through it. Never noticing the strange man outside her gates digging threw the trash, watching her every move. Twinnie notices a red, white, and blue envelope, dated April 20, 1999. It was from the United States Land Surveyor Office. She opened the letter curious to see what they wanted. Walking back to the house her blood pressure was boiling, knowing they want to take her land. This was the third attempt, but this time it came straight from the president's office.

Walking to her study closing the door, Twinnie sits down and takes a deep breath. Terrell her husband pops from out of her body. I can't believe the nerve of that no good Prez Burnt, said Terrell. Don't stress he says my Shettiamour! Terrell starts massaging her legs, rubbing her feet and sucking her toes. Twinnie laughs saying you know I love it when you tickle me, my caring Humpkin.

Dam! Are we ever allowed to have anything as black people? "Said Twannie." This land holds all our ancestors from the 1800's until now. Don't worry my Shettiamour they'er never take this land. If the powder cakes do they will just suffer the consequences! They laughed thinking if they knew what was good for them, the president and his kind would leave this land alone.

The children were knocking at the study door calling for mom. They're dad answers asking,'what do you want?' Both children talking at the same time, shouting about what each other can't do. Mom hollers Q-time right now! You Bams! Where are your manners? Now one at a time, I can't hear when you two are squeaking and squealing at the same time. Her daughter Riaz spoke first explaining how they're science reports were due soon. Royal her son said we have no clue on the subject, what shall we make? You two better use those crome-domes you were graced with. Turn on the lightbulbs, you can create anything. Royal said, I will make a beauty cream that transforms you for 24 hours. Riaz laughed saying I will make a plant grow fully in 48 hours. Twinnie and Terell said we knew you could do it, we believe in you. Now get busy you brainiacs, love you. Terrell said I'm quite sure y'all can surprise everybody. Oh before I forget don't worry bout the letter. I will see you later my Shettiamour! Terell stood up and merged back into Twinnie.

Early morning arrived the children were rushing getting ready for school. After grabbing a quick brak-fast they get into the limo and was driven to school. Twinnie ready for the day looking beautiful as ever. The doorbell rings, Twinnie thinking who could that be this early in the day? Lester the wallet molester BKA the butler. Lester was wearing his favorite diamond shaped glass-es. A painted on tux tie tee shirt, with black slacks. He walks to the door, opens it saying "who the hell rang my dam bell? Oh it was you? It was you? He approaches the strange lady, throws her arms up into the air. He then pats her down and lifts her wallet from her purse. Lester moves so quickly and smoothly, she never notices her wallet missing.

Lester announces on the radio a Mrs. Hogger to see you Mrs. Twinnie. She utters the secret code [tunnels], said Twinnie! For him to usher her into the office. Lester ushers Mrs. Hogger into the corridor, leading her down the hallway. Their parrot Wenbone sits in a large cage in the middle of he hallway. Wenbone says" argh, come in mother-fucker leave your wallet at the door, sit your ass on the floor!" "Ha, ha, ha, ha laughs Wenbone." Mrs. Hogger says "oh what an amusing bird! Their parrot says "yo mama amused all the pirates! "Hoe- chops is her name". Ha, ha, ha, ha! I'm not a bird, I"m a mighty man says Wenbone!

Lester enters Twinnie office announcing Mrs.Hogger. Twinnie offers her a seat, asking what is the reason for your trespass on my land? I know you saw the big sign? Trespass at your own risk! Mrs. Hogger answered saying you can call me Amber. I am here to survey the land. "Oh the land not my land?" Twinnie said.

Mrs. Hogger puts her briefcase on top of the desk, then opens it. She reached in it pulling out the survey papers. Amber hands Twinnie a

copy to keep. I have to conduct a survey consist-
ing of measurements and mineral tests. Twinnie
says to her, you think that because you're the
government you can come and just take our
land? Amber says President Burnt wants this
done immediately today. I have my crew and in-
struments outside and we will be conducting the
survey. She stood up looking at Lester to usher
her out. Twinnie nodded her head looking at
Lester. He escorts Amber to the door. He said to
her leave and never return, you trespassing itch
scratch!

Amber walks over to her crew who were already
setting up. She was thinking what a weird "O"!
The butler! As they were setting everything in
place for the first test, the ground rumbles and
shakes. The crew looks at each other then the
ground beneath them opens up! Everything and
everyone falls into one big hole. The hole quickly closes up like nothing ever happened. The
crew landed safely falling beneath the earth,
into a cave with several chambers. The surveyors didn't know which way to go. They were so
confused and shocked hollering at each other
trying to figure out how to get out. Everyone

was so frightened they ran in different directions.

Twinnie was still in the house sitting at her desk, thinking how Amber insisted on the survey. The nerve of her what a assnoid! Terrell emerges saying,"don't worry my Shettiamour I am here for you. He starts massaging her legs then caressing her feet, and kissing her toes. My Shettiamour, Shettiamour forever Shettiamour! Twinnie changed the subject talking, about the kids surprise 16th party. Don't forget, there new cars will be delivered next week. Yes great distraction the race, then the surprise birthday party. I love the new track you had built, on the east side of our property. What a great idea they have no clue about the surprise carnival , Said Terrell. You know it has to be a spectacular event as always, Humpkin. Whoever wins the race get their car first! Great idea we have one week to get the carnival and race accomplished. Terrell said, that's a brilliant idea. They will enjoy driving in front of their relatives and friends.

Terrell stopped rubbing her feet. He stood up and said, you know I must go now. I have things to do. Twinnie said, you always have things to do, always a busy man. What's the diff? I'll be back when your family arrives. You know they'll be here soon? If they keep coming after our land. Yeah said Twinnie. There's only one person I want to see it's auntie Tyinnie. Who I was named after. She spells her name with the Y instead of a W like mine. I miss her. Terrell kisses Twinnie and pops back into her. I have to get prepared, everyone's coming. Twinnie calls for Cruddexter the foot. She she gives him instructions to inform the staff of her upcoming plans. Cruddexter puts on his bowtie and tap dancing shoes. He taps to her staff, get every room ready our family is coming for a visit. Currently behind-the-scenes the land surveyors, are running , scared, and confused in the underground tunnels.

The children return home from school. They run and hug their mother. She asked them about their homework. They both answered saying we're on it mom. Riaz and Royal grab a snack, then start they're homework. While, at the table, they were talking to each other about their upcoming birthday. Riaz asked Royale do you think we're gonna have a party this year? Royale answered saying he did not know? He was snooping and did not find any evidence of a surprise party. Riaz said maybe they're too busy with the land. Plus all the relatives are coming. Don't worry said Royal. I don't care about the land. It's my birthday they better give, or do something! See that's why you're a Bam always demanding. Said Riaz.

The doorbell rings Lester gets up, walking to the door. He opens the door and asked "who the hell rang my damn bell?" Oh! It was you? It was you? Tyinnie where did you come from? He tries to throw her arms up in the air. She slapped him across his head with her zerpurse. Let loose my zerpurse you thiefests. Not today you won't be thefting my wallet. Ah-line your-self Lester, step to the left you thiefest Said Tyinnie. You know my grandson Malachi, right? He could stay in the room with his cousin Royale. Take him to his cousin so we can get saturated. Hi, how you doing today? Said Lester. He chirped Royale, come down here and and get your Cuz man. Yeah Malachi says, Unk I heard about you. What you be doing with those wallets? (Lester in his mind picturing how, he drops the wall in his room every night and admires his library full of wallets). Lester paused, then said come on here you little Bam. Hey wallet, molester, you can take me to my niece Twinnie. "Yeah you got the right name Lester the wallet molester! Said Tyinnie. You better keep your damn hands to yourself. My wallet come up missing, you're gonna; be missing teeth, hands, a body, all that! You just remember all that! Tyinnie was waving her hands up-and-down, and all around him, all that missing!"

Little Twinnie walks towards auntie Tyinnie. Stops in front of her and blows her a kiss. Auntie catches it, wow! Necie Pooh You've been doing that since you was a little girl. Blowing me a kiss. Is it because you got that man, husband, thang inside of you? Or you just don't want no woman hugging on him? While laughing, I don't blame you.   Chald, that husband of yours make a woman lust and thangs, almost combust. Come on Chald we need to be chappin, before everyone gets here. Get caught up and thangs.

They walked into the city room together. Auntie

can I get you anything to drink? Cha you can get me a cold Jamaican fruit drink. Since I feel like I'm in Jamaica in this room. I'm waiting for you to open up them plato doors; and the tide rolls on in rolling us unto the beach! I should've put my swamsuite on; since we are in Jamaica that's all. Hurry up oped those Plato doors! Auntie laughing. That's all I'm saying it's nice to be in Jamaica.

Necie Pooh are you ready for the change to come? Yes auntie no matter what, me Terrell and the kids are ready. Did you tell the kids? I had to considering this matter is so pressing, the president wanting our land. Chad went shall everybody else arrives? I think tomorrow, auntie, that's what all the notices say. Everybody knows about the deed that's why they are coming for support. Yeah, yeah I got my bestest suit ready said auntie.

The children come into the room, speaking to auntie. Yeah y'all has grown like links since last I saw y'all. Handsome and beautiful, my necie can't be your mama auntie laughing. Too good looking you know. Y'all got your good looks from auntie. The children stare at her and laugh, running from the city room. Twinnie picked up the radio and told the children to get ready for bed after dinner. My what? Do you have a radio for chappin with your children? Is this house that jynormous? Yeah, that way they can't say they didn't hear me; and I don't have to be hollering. Yeah like some ghetto wreck. I have a radio for everyone who's coming. Here's yours, auntie. Do you know how to work it? Old as I am, I better know how to work some- thing! Twinnie laughed. Auntie you know where your room is? It's getting late, and to- morrow will be a long day. I'm going to party with Mr. Silky. Love you good night.a1`

Chapter 2

The Surveyor

It was Friday morning. The children were leaving for school. They had a big break-fast. Twinnie was waiting for her auntie to come down and eat with her. However, auntie did not come until 9 AM. She was still stretching and yawning. I couldn't even open my shutters this morning. She said laughing. The doorbell rings. I wonder who's coming next, tell them to meet me at the break-fast table.

Lester goes and answered the door. He says "who the hell rang my damn bell?" It was his dad Desmeir. His dad shouted "get back, stand back, before you get smacked trying to jack!" Don't try to work me down! You won't be levitating my wallet today. Just take my items to my room. I'm going to get fresh for break-fast. Wenbone the bird said as they were coming towards him. "Come here motherfucker leave your wallet at the door, sit your ass on the floor! Argh, ha, ha, ha, laughed Wenbone. Desmeir says "I'm not leaving you zilt." I will shoot you

in the head with a rubber band! Wenbone said
Argh "I'll kick you in the ass with my foot."
What a bird, said Des. Your mama is a crazy
bird! Your mama is a crazy bird!   Lester
grabbed his dad's luggage, laughing at Wenbone.
Never mind that bird, let's go to your room dad.

Before Lester could get down the stairs, the
doorbell rang again. He hurries to the door, saying who the hell rang my damn bell? Oh it was
you? It was you?   Lester looking at the two sis-
ters. Simultaneously they said "get your dead
paws back you fly." You won't be clutching our
zerpurses today. Kareem said. I'll be watching
you Lester! Caroline ask where is our niece?
While walking through the hallway. Wenbone
said Argh . "Come here, ladies, Argh listen.
Come in motherfucker leave your wallet at the
door, sit your ass on the floor! Argh, ha, ha, ha
Wenbone laughing. Caroline said where did you
get that thing from? If it's not Lester, robbing
you, it's a crazy bird. Look at him sis! Look at
his clothes! What bird wears ripped up jeans, a
pirate hat and a patch on his eye, said Caroline?
He must think he's a pirate. Is that why he
wants to rob you, for your wallet? Laughed Ka-

reem. Where is our necie Kareem said? Does she know we are here? Lester show them to their room and waited for them. After getting settled in Kareem, rushed into the hallway, almost knocking over Lester. Excited about meeting with their siblings. Lester told them everyone's meeting at break-fast this way, hell y'all know the way. Yeah you old dusters he mumbled under his breath. Caroline asked, what did you say? Lester answer oh nothing as he was walking away.

Everyone was seated at the table when Kareem and Caroline arrived. Twinnie and Terrell was on one end, auntie Tyinnie was at the other end. Everyone else sat across from each other in the middle, including Lester. Kareem ask Lester why are you here? Lester answered, see it's people like you who gets ignored. What you forgot my role would change also. I can't wait! (Lester dreaming inside his head all the new people he can steal their wallets.)

Can I get everyone's attention please? Auntie Tyinnie said. This is not the official meeting today. It's just a reminder for you to review your upcoming positions in life. However, the meeting will be tomorrow, at lunch. After Terrell"s grandparents arrive. Be prepared to rehearse your upcoming position. Prez Burnt will force Twinnie and Terrell to sign the deed. I don't know about you, but I didn't vote for President Burnt, said Caroline. Those powder cakes will get what they have coming said Desmire. Let the world turn!

What's on the agenda Necie Pooh? First off, welcome home fam. I missed everyone and I hope you enjoy being here. The bams birthday party will be this up coming weekend. We're having a car race between the bams and a carnival. It's a surprise, so no one says anything to them. Terrell said wow! I'm surprised now the track is finished! One task complete says Twinnie. We're going to go see the track in a few. Twinnie said. I'm not gonna sit on no hard bench, said Caroline. Twinnie (swayed her hand) I beg your pardon, I'm not a chime-dime like you! Only the most comfortable plush seating, for the Ad-Dam's! Twinnie rolled her eyes at auntie Caroline. (Twinnie was thinking her aunt is so pennyish, She squeaks when she thinks of spending.)   Also we will be taking a fam photo on Monday after lunch. The colors we can vote on at dinner tonight. OK, everybody just keep your mind on the situation says Des.

Oh, before I forget, Lester give everyone a radio said Twinnie. Caroline said, a radio what"s that for? Ah, to keep in touch! You know we're not into those radioactive phones? Giving you breast cancer, brain, cancer, cancer, any other cancer! Besides my bams, don't need all that technology; they enjoy making things. They make robots and drones. Everyone be careful when driving around the property. Please don't run over any of the small drones. They look like birds, trees, aliens, rocks, you know, how bams think. All right come on everybody. Let's go see the racetrack. Meet me at the garage said Twinnie.

Everyone was gathering around the golf carts admiring them. Kareem said, wow these look much better than those golf cart you had before. Can we drive these on the street? Yes Twinnie said, you can drive them to the mall, they go up to 55 mph. We're gonna have fun this weekend, said Tyinnie. Yes, that's the birthday spirit keep it up yeah. Hey I know this blue one is for me, and my extra long legs? SAID Tyinnie. No, auntie it"s that red one over there! Oh you funny I'll be riding around like a big red bug; hanging on a tree. Stop it auntie yours is custom made for you. I put the diamond in the back, a TV antenna with the white walls. Come on y'all follow me to the track. Last one to the tracks have to feed the captives. No let them starve serves them right, said Caroline. Oh you have always been a crude duster said Des. Enough fam let's go on the track, and have some fun said Twinnie. Everyone's name is etched on their seats. Latter that evening Kareem had to feed the captives. She had her brother Des help out.

Monday morning everyone is at break-fast, chappin about the up coming events. The bell rings, Lester answers the door. "Who the hell rang my dam bell?" Oh it was you? It was you? SaLester asked. While he throws the man arms into the air patting him down. I'm John Hurybutt from the United Stated Land Survey Office. Lester ask what do you want? While patting him down and stealing his wallet. I'm here to survey the land, said Mr. Hurybutt. Lester chirps Cruddexter to tell Twannie about the land server. Lester beckons for the man to follow him. Come here, come here, I got a secret! Argh," come in motherfucker leave your wallet at the door; sit your ass on the floor." Ha, ha, ha, ha, said Wenbone. John said wow what a bird! Wenbone says, your mom's a crazy bird!

In Twinnie's office Cruddexter dressed in his tap dance shoe and bowtie. He just finished tapping the message concerning the new surveyor at the house. Just as he was finishing Lester and John arrive at Twinnie's office. Have a seat she said. "How can I help you today? Don't play innocent, John said. What happened to the other surveyors who was here before me? You know I'm out here to survey this land. Twinnie answered saying, "I truly don't know where the other surveyors could be!" Twinnie said, oh what is her name? Amber right? Yes said John. I told her the same thing that I am telling you. Do your job Hurybutt and get the hell off my land!

Hey hell-butt this way, Lester gestured pointing and escorting him to the door. John was outside finally he walked over to his team. They were already performing the first test. What a strange bunch, John thought. All of a sudden the ground started to shake. The earth opened up and swallowed everything and everybody. The equipment and crew went tumbling down into the tunnels. They all were hollering for help! The earth quickly closed, everything recovered as though nothing ever happened. Twinnie and Lester were watching and laughing. Your the only one who is never seen or heard. She said. Don't forget to feed the captives Twinnie said. Ya see that's what powder cakes get, being so insentience. Said Lester. You mean instance? Don;t be cojecting my e-bonicts, said Lester.

Chapter 3

The Birthday Race

Early Friday morning Riaz, Royal, and Malachi were up chappin. They had their own private channel separate from the adults. Excited and anxious how they could race and win a car. Malachi said on the radio, "I don't care who wins the race I'm breezing the car first. Happy Birthday y'all! You don't have a DL permit, how you summing? Laughed Royal. Riaz was laughing claiming her victory in the race. You know I breeze better than you Royal and Mal put together! Plus its my Birthday! You mean our birthday, said Royal. Mal said to Royal "sorry cuz Riaz is going to win! Cross-dust that's all you'll be winning, said Royal! Let's go y'all the last one to the tract already lost. Somehow they all arrived at the same time, parking there ATV's.

They ran over to the tract screaming about the flaming race cars. They look around the tract and notice unique plush seating. All their relatives seated in plush chairs, built like stadium seating on steroids. Their is four race cars, a black with red stripes, a blue with red stripes, a red with black stripes and a purple with orange stripes. Mal screams this is so hype man! The first race is between the twins. Uncle Des tells them to pick a car to race. He then explains the three lap race to them. Don't forget you drive two laps to warm up, said uncle Des.

Raiz and Royal run over to there cars. Royal picked the blue and Raiz picked the purple one. They take off with excitement, racing down the track. After the two laps, Mal parks his car. The twins line up at the start line Uncle Des waves the flag zoom they went! Royal is in the lead, for the first two laps. Here comes Raiz breezin pushing to catch up to Royal All of a sudden after a curve they are running bumper to bumper! All their relatives jump up with excitement cheering them on. The race is getting tighter they are still bumper to bumper in the final lap! They cross over the finish line as Mal waves the flag. They park the cars get out anxious to find out who won. Unk Des declared the race was a tie between the twins.

Mal was ready to race the twins to show off his

driving skills. They were breezin all afternoon until dusk. Twinnie wanted to make sure they return to the house without wondering around. She radioed them claiming that she sprang her ankle, thus having to go to the hospital. The bams drove home as planned, they walked into the house. There dad said she is out on the patio, come help her before the ambulance arrive. They rushed to the back paito doors.

Blinded by a bunch of flashing lights glaring through the glass doors. They were thinking the ambulance had arrived. Royal opened the doors for his sister. "Surprise everyone shouted, Happy Birthday!" The twins were stoked, all their school friends, neighbors, and relatives were there. Cruddexter was tapping in his red glimmering tux, black tap shoe and birthday hat. Tap, tap, tap {Happy Birthday} he tapped! Wenbone dressed in his red water trunks and birthday tie. He was repeating Happy Birthday Bam's I love you! They saw carnival games, food booths, and water rides.

The twins were playing games with their friends having a bomb of a time. Suddenly they heard "check one, check, two will the birthday bams; come to the center of the carnival?" They stoped and ran to the center, not knowing what to expect. In the middle of the carnival behind the games and booths. Their grandparents sitting under an arch covered with balloons. Sitting in plush throne like chairs holding birthday balloons smiling. There was a large black tarp with Happy Birthday written on it and two huge red bows. Royal and Ritz ran over to the tarp curious to see what was under it. Mom and dad approached them with mic's in their hands. Dad said I know you want to open this one first, "Happy Birthday my bams we love you!" The twins immediately started unwrapping the tarp. There sat two 1999 mustang cars, and and a mountain of presents. Royal said "walkaflaka, walkaflaka, mom and dad! Raiz said to her Bff who was standing next to her; "I'm too stoked!' Mom handed Royal his new keys. Dad handed Raiz her keys. Dad said, y'all know they come with rules, and a curfews. Don't get it locked down said mom. The twins were truly stoked! Hollering and dancing thanks mom, dad and everyone. Riaz ran to her purple mustang with orange stripes. Royal ran to his black mustang with red stripes. Malachi said, this is the bomb party with slamming gifts! I can't wait to turn sixteen. The music was blasting the lights were glaring. The party did't end until after 3am. The twins fell asleep in there new cars.

Chapter 4

President Burnt Of The United States

Three days left and spring break would be over. The twins were up early stoked, waiting for there parents to take them driving. Finally 10:00am everyone was up and eating break-fast chappin about the birthday. Happy as everyone was they knew life was going to change. They were laughing and joking, knowing what was going to happen. Terrell says "well I hope everybody's ready for there new role in life. It was just a matter of time, waiting for the powder cakes to take our land. I don't know about y'all but, I have to prepare for the science fair thats today. Said Twinnie If anyone wants to go be ready in 30.

Riaz was fussing with her hair, but her science project was ready. She invented a new weedy seed that grows into a full plant in 48 hours. Riaz had her project staged into four different plants explaining their growth. Royal was up fussing about his project. He needed someone to demonstrate on. Terell called for Lester on the radio. Get ready man you are gonna be the genie pig at the fair for the children. Lester was furious he had no ideal what the cream would do to him.

Upton there arrival at the science fair. Lester says to Royal man just on't make me look like some crazy animal, alien or monster! Trust me Unk, this cream only makes you look better you will see! Raiz set her project, the judges were admiring how rapid the plants grew. Royal was the last contestant he anxiously awaited. Finally when the judge arrived he applied the cream on Lesters face. Holler ah, said Lester!

What is that? Asked one of the judges. He looks so handsome, what a transformation! One judge said to the other. Everyone was amazed the cream worked. It lasts for 24 hours, said Royal. Twinnie had taken photos before and after the cream was applied. People started surrounding them asking where can they get some of that cream. People were trying to grab the cream and his information. His dad had Wenbone on his shoulders. Wenbone started flapping his wings, saying "back up you vultures no cream for you! Get back, step back before you get wamacked! Said Wenbone. The judges parted the crowd, trying to announce the winner. They crowned Royal 1st place and Raiz second place. They presented Royal with a trophy and a one thousand dollar check. Raiz won a second place trophy and five hundred dollars. Twinnie started packing up the children's projects, with Lesters help. Everyone was so amazed with Royal's project they had to flee the gym. In the limo mom said this is as bad as the president wanting to take our land. Don't worry said Terell, the land always take care of itself. Lester was holding a mirror looking at himself in disbelief. You say 24 hours ,man you are a genius. You better hide there inventions, the world will come after them. Dam I look good! Yeah don't I look good he kept saying. Let me get that cream man Lester said. Royal was laughing saying don't forget to feed the captives. Thats your beauty cream!

Arriving at the estate Twinnie and Terell go to there bedroom to put the inventions into the safe. The alarm alerts them someone is at the front gates. They look on the cameras then the bell rings.

Ring, ring the doorbell rings. Twinnie tells Lester and Cruddexter to answer the bell. Lester opens the door and asks,"who the hell rang my dam bell? Oh it was you? It was you? He reaches out grabbing the man. The man grabs Lester's arm, swing him around and put him in a headlock. FBI he says now back off, as he releases him. He never knew Lester stole his wallet. Conduct yourself said the FBI man. I am with the President he is here to throw you off his land. You can't pat me down! Lester laughs at him saying, wow you powder cakes have a lot of big Buda balls! Lester announced on the radio, Prez Burnt is here. That's President Burnt not Prez said the man! Cruddexter steps on the man's foot with force. The agent hollered in pain looking down at a foot steeping on his foot! "What the Hell is this?" Cruddexter scurries into the house tapping a message to Twinnie on the radio. Tap, tap, tap President Burnt and his body dummies are here with three car lodes of dummies with blazers. When they walked passed Wenbone he says, your name is Burnt caus you escaped out of hell! Argh Burnt escaped from hell, ha, ha, ha, ha. You're gonna get it! Twinnie is in her room, Terell pops back out of her. He says see you in your office running out the bedroom door.

Lester is forced to escort them to Twinnie and Terell. Glad to see you are so confident Mr. Burnt Buzzard! Said Lester. The other body dummies gather the AD-Dam fam together in the dinning room. Holding them at blaze point. Grandpa says were not afraid of you weaklings!. "You'r nothing but cowards!" Grandpa says yeah "if you didn't have those blazers I would kick hell out of you!" Grandma says, "I would whip you like your mother should have whipped you 20 years ago! Then you would have some respect." Auntie Tyinnie puts a tablecloth on her body dummies head while Cruddexter kicks him in the leg. She runs out the room into her niece; in the hallway being escorted to her office.

One of the other FBI men whispered to his partner; "who are these weird people? What have we gotten our selves into? Listening to the president, hope we good man said his partner! President Burnt with his bodacious attitude, insisting that he will have our land. In Twinnie's office they were holding Terell, Lester, and Des. Escorted to her office finally, two bode dummies were surrounding her door. Twinnie said, I don't know what you use to! However, "this is my house move your wanna be important selves out of my way!" My Shettiamour has arrived, said Terell. Prez Burnt orders his men to go get the children. Terell says, "what my children have to do with this?" Leave the children alone! Prez Burnt waves his hand at his body dummies and says "go get them! Twinnie hurries and radios to the children, asking them to come to the office. She tells prez Brunt "Don't put your hands on my children, while leaping forward towards him!" Her husband grabs her saying let me handle this my Shettiamour! You are from hell! Said auntie Tyinnie.

When the children arrive, Prez Burnt threatens to kill them. Twinnie jumps in front of them, shouting at the Prez. "What kind of infected crime grime dog are you? Coming to our estate treating to kill us and our children for our land. Terell jumps in front of Twinnie and the kids. He says to Prez Burnt, "Have your men put those blazers down away from my fam! Then I will shread you from existence with your….. Auntie Tyinnie has to hold Terell back. Don't worry, remember necie and nephew time tells on everyone! All the powder cakes are gonna get it. Watch, he asked for it now give it to them.

Cruddexter was in his tap shoe box on Twinnie's desk. He steps out onto her desk wearing tap shoes with spikes, and a rambar in front of his shoe. He taps there gonna get it! He returns to his sneaker box. The FBI men looked at each other with fear. Burnt said I don't care what that was, if it reappears blaze it! Wenbone parched on Terell's shoulder says, "argh y'all gonna get it! Ha, ha, ha just you wait and see!

"Let's get to the issue at hand, sign the dam deed people and get off my land he shouted!" You are going to sign that dam deed now! Or my men will kill you and your family! Auntie Tyinnie snapped back.   Stood up walking towards Prez Burnt. Saying let the **B** to the **L** to the **A** to the **C** to the **K** people rang in-power! Tyinnie points her finger in Prez Burnt's face. She says all you powder cakes is going to get what's coming to you!   Twinnie said leave my children out of this!   Sign the dam deed or else, said President Burnt!   There will be no witness. No one will know!   I'am the President of the United States!   See what a good job can get you, ha, ha, ha, ha.   I'll burn this house down with y'all in it!   Terell walks over to the safe opens it with his voice.   He grabs the deed and place it on the desk.   He looks at Twinnie, they look at auntie Tyinnie.   She looks at Unk Des, they all look at the deed and agree.   Twinnie and Terell sign the deed together.   Auntie Tyinnie says, "Let the world turn!"   Terell hands it to Prez Brunt. The president snatches the document, hollering now get the Hell off my land.   You have two days to get out of my house.   Every thing you leave will be singed, Burnt laughing.

Don't worry you will be all alone, soon enough! The Ad-Dam Fam laughs.   He was upset and asked; why are you laughing so much when I just took your land and everything you own? Dam you AD-Dam's!   Just get off my land!   Said President Burnt.   Auntie Tyinnie laughs real loud and says " you're gonna get it!   You just waits and see!

The president was so confident having the deed in his hands. He immediately decided to return to the white housed to gather his things. He was thinking all the tunnels no one will know when I come and go. It will be my ideal hang out for me and my women. Who has the biggest Buda Balls now! Him and his body dummies get into the three limos. As they are exiting the property, they notice the gates are closed. Prez Burnt speaks on the intercom demanding that they get out and open those dam gates. Out of nowhere all the limos windows roll down. The deed burns prez Burnt hands. He lets it go and it flies out of the window up into the air.

Prez Burnt he shouts get that deed! However, no one can get out of the limos. He watches it fly up into the air. He sees a golden flame changing the name on the deed, back to the AD-Dam Fam. Before he could utter a word the ground started rumbling and shaking. The earth opens up and all three limos fall beneath it. They were screaming for help! The ground quickly closes up with no sings of disturbance. All the Ad-Dam Fam said simultaneously, we told you! You're gonna get it! Ha, ha, ha, ha!

Scene One

Retribution

President Brunt, his surveyors and all his body dummies are incarcerated at ADXW Florence. Wearing black and white stripes with a ball and chain. Burnt is holding onto the bars hollering out! "I'am the president of the United States let me out you fools.

This is BPTU {Black People Television United.} Breaking New Report "Today in the news, there's a crazy powder cake in jail hollering. "I Quote " "I'am President Burnt let me out!" "I don't belong here". However Blanton Burnt is in jail for life!   Burnt is the head of the Singed Cartel organization. He has been charged with seven counts of murder in the 1st degree, and major drug trafficking! Him and all the members of his cartel. Well as we all know thats the last of the Singed Carte

Scene Two

Crowning Glory

Good afternoon I'am Paula Spike from BPTU News of Washington D.C., were we report the current events all around the world. In todays news, it's the 40th anniversary the day Beckie Fishbone a powder cake who refuse to sit at the back of the bus. We have a special live report, coming from the capital. Lets go live with Hershey Ruth. This is Hershey Ruth reporting live at the Black House here in Washington. As you can see and hear the powder cakes came from across the world. Gathering to protest for equality and civil rights. The crowd is getting angry and out of control the national guard has ben called in. Stay tuned in for the latest developments! [In the background people burning sings throwing rocks at the Black House; shouting we want equality!

Scene Three

President Tyinnie AD-Dam

Hello America this is Reporter Jake Wealth reporting live from the Black House. Today's special report from Our President Tyinnie AD-Dam of the United States of America.

Good afternoon my fellow American'ts! I Tyinnie AD-Dam as your Prez. Pray for all and every Powder Cake citizen facing the results of the Civil Rights Act. Bill CRA-211 it has been vetoed by congress. I will not oppose there decision, it shall be held in agreement. Good Nite. {Reporters asking questions in the background.} Prez AD-Dam exits the stage.

Reporter Jake Wealth here inside the Black House. You heard it here first on BPTU the CRA-211 bill has been vetoed by congress and the President will up-hold there decision. Back to you Paula.

THE END!

Made in the USA
Columbia, SC
16 November 2024

46565711R00022